# HEAL

# A HEALTH AND WELLNESS GUIDE TO THE INTERNET

Second Edition

WCB/McGraw-Hill

Boston   Burr Ridge, IL   Dubuque, IA   Madison, WI
New York   San Francisco   St. Louis
Bangkok   Bogotá   Caracas   Lisbon   London   Madrid   Mexico City
Milan   New Delhi   Seoul   Singapore   Sydney   Taipei   Toronto

## WCB/McGraw-Hill
*A Division of The McGraw-Hill Companies*

HEALTH NET: A HEALTH AND WELLNESS GUIDE TO THE INTERNET, SECOND EDITION

Copyright ©1999 by The McGraw-Hill Companies, Inc. All rights reserved. Printed in the United States of America.

The contents of, or parts thereof, may not be reproduced in any form for any other purpose without permission of the publisher..

This book is printed on recycled paper containing 10% postconsumer waste.

1 2 3 4 5 6 7 8 9 0 DOC/DOC 9 0 9 8

ISBN 0-07-228839-6

www.mhhe.com

# CONTENTS

## Part I: Internet Primer   1

Introduction   1

What is the Internet?   1

Getting Started on the Internet   1

Electronic Mail (E-mail)   3

World Wide Web (WWW)   4

Tips for Using the World Wide Web   8

Listservs   9

Newsgroups/Usenet   10

FTP   12

Netiquette   13

Doing Research with the Internet   14

Thinking Critically about Health Information on the Internet   15

## Part II: Internet Resources for Health and Wellness   17

General Health Information   17

Aging   20

AIDS and HIV   22

Alcohol   24

Birth Control and Abortion   26

Cancer  28

Cardiovascular Health  30

Death and Dying  32

Environmental Health  34

Exercise and Fitness  36

The Health Care System  38

Mental Health  40

Nutrition  42

Pregnancy and Childbirth  45

Psychoactive Drugs  47

Sexuality  49

Sexually Transmitted Diseases  51

Stress  53

Tobacco  55

Weight Management and Eating Disorders  57

# INTERNET PRIMER

## Introduction

It seems like you can't open a newspaper without seeing an article about the Internet. Even billboards have companies' Web addresses listed at the bottom. But what is the Internet, and how is it useful to you? This booklet is designed to give you a practical introduction to the Internet, and to provide you with health-related resources on the Net. These resources will help you as you take your health class, and they may also be valuable to you in the future if you or someone you know needs information about a health topic.

Many people believe that learning to navigate on the Internet is difficult or time-consuming. That's just not true. Once you are in front of a computer with Internet capabilities, using e-mail or surfing the Web is no harder than using a word processor. You don't have to be a computer expert to utilize the Internet. All you need is a little curiosity and the desire to communicate and share information with others.

## What is the Internet?

The Internet is a global web connecting more than a million computers in over 70 countries around the world. The Internet is decentralized, and there is little regulation over its use. Computers are connected through phone lines linked to servers and hosts in strategic places. The most popular uses of the Internet now are electronic mail (e-mail) and the World Wide Web.

## Getting Started on the Internet

In order to log on to the Internet, you need a properly equipped computer, a modem, and access to an Internet Service Provider.

## Equipment

Most colleges and universities have computers available to students in labs or in the library. These are often hooked up to the Internet, and there is probably a knowledgeable person nearby to help you log on and answer any questions. If you want to set up your own personal computer system with Internet access, you'll need the following equipment:

- a computer
- a modem
- a telephone line (You can use your regular telephone line which will cause a busy signal when you are online, or you can get a "dedicated line"—a separate phone line just for Internet access.)
- an Internet Service Provider (ISP)

## Modems

A modem is a piece of equipment that changes the information that a computer works with into the kind of information that can be passed over the telephone lines. It is what allows your computer to "talk" to other computers around the world. It can be an external unit or an internal card that is placed in the hard drive. Most new computers now come with built-in modems.

Modems come in different speeds. The speed of a modem determines how quickly information can be downloaded or accessed from the Internet. At this time, the most widely used speed is 33.6; however, modems are continually getting faster.

## Internet Service Providers

Most colleges and universities provide Internet access to their students and faculty at a reasonable cost, and if you have access to this you should probably use it. But if you need to hook up a computer to the Internet on your own, you must go through an Internet Service Provider (ISP). ISPs are companies that run the computers that enable you to get onto the Net; these computers are called servers. It works like this: when you log onto the Net your modem dials your ISP. When the modem is connected to the ISP, it actually connects to their modem on their computer (the computer at the ISP is called the server). The best-known ISPs are national ones like America On-Line and Microsoft Network. But there are many smaller ISPs out there as well.

There are a few considerations to keep in mind in choosing among the many ISPs:

- Cost - Do they have a flat fee for unlimited Internet time each month, or will they charge you for each minute you are on-line? Some services have several different plans you can choose from; the best one for you depends on how much time you spend on-line each month. Be sure to shop around and find an ISP that offers you the best rate plan for you.
- Traffic - Some ISPs get a lot of traffic and it can be difficult to get online (particularly the larger, national companies). Find out the "dial up" number (the number your modem calls to link up) of an ISP and call it at different times during the day to see if it's busy.
- Service - Some ISPs are courteous and prompt in answering customer questions and complaints; others have trouble in this area. Ask your friends and acquaintances for recommendations of ISPs that have good service.

## **Electronic Mail (E-mail)**

E-mail is a way of transmitting messages across a phone line to a specified other person's computer. To send or receive e-mail you must have a program called a mail browser (some common ones are Eudora and Microsoft Mail) and an e-mail account. When you send an e-mail to someone, you type in his or her e-mail address at the top. E-mail addresses consist of the individual user's name or identification, the @ symbol, and the name of their server and domain: username@servername.domainname.

After writing your message in the "body" of the e-mail, you can send it. The message is transmitted across phone lines to the recipient server which "sorts" the mail and sends it to the individual's e-mail address.

E-mail is generally somewhat informal and not very lengthy. E-mail can be used for everything from sending out memos, keeping up with friends and relatives, telecommuting, and exchanging documents and files.

Here are a few things to keep in mind about using e-mail:

- Try to check your mail every day, especially if you belong to a mailing list (see section on listservs). It's amazing how quickly your "mailbox" can fill up with messages.
- Know your netiquette (see page 12).
- Don't send anything too confidential or sensitive over e-mail; e-mail is easily accessed by others.
- Proofread your e-mail before you send it.

*Exercise*: Find a buddy who also has an e-mail account. Try experimenting with some features of your mail browser with your buddy. Can you forward a message from someone else to your buddy? Can you store a whole group of e-mail addresses and then send the same message to all of them? Can you attach a document from a word processor to your e-mail message so your buddy can retrieve and read it?"

_____

_____

_____

_____

## World Wide Web (WWW)

Since 1992 when the World Wide Web was first launched, it has exploded into mainstream culture. For many people the Internet has become synonymous with the Web. The Web is a gold mine of information on just about any topic you can think of, and more is being added every day. As technology becomes more sophisticated, Web sites are starting to feature animation, video, and sound, and by the time you read this there will probably be many more exciting innovations.

**Browsers**

To get to the World Wide Web you have to have a computer program called a Web browser. Some of the better-known and popular Web browsers are Netscape and Microsoft Internet Explorer. You can purchase a browser from a computer store, get one from your ISP, or download one from the Web itself. Once you are logged on to the Internet, you simply click to open the browser and you are ready to surf the Net.

**Web Addresses**

The Web is made up of millions of websites (or webpages). Each website has an address, which is known as the URL (which stands for Uniform Resource Locator). A typical URL looks like this: http://www.mhhe.com. This is the address for the McGraw-Hill Higher Education Publishing Company website. To get to any website, all you have to do is type in the URL in your Web browser.

You can analyze a website address to figure out who and what they are.

- "http" stands for HyperText Transport Protocol; it is the language of the Web.
- generally you will see "www" which tells the server that we want to get our information from the World Wide Web.
- the last two parts of the address are called the domain name. The "domain" indicates what kind of site it is. In our case it is ".com" (pronounced dot-com) which stands for "commercial". Other domains you will probably come across include: ".edu" = education, ".org" = organization, and ".gov" = government. When you read the address for a

website out loud, remember that every "." is pronounced "dot."

*Exercise:* What can you guess about the following websites based on their addresses?

http://www.oncolink.upenn.edu

http://www.runnersworld.com

http://www.lungusa.org/main.html

gopher://gopher.nih.gov

_____

_____

_____

_____

_____

**Surfing the Web**

A key concept to understand in surfing the Web is "links." Links are highlighted words or images on a web page that you can click on to go to other pages. Once you find a topic that interests you, it is easy to explore just by clicking on links. Keep in mind that some links will connect you to another page by the same organization; others will take you to another site completely.

A person or organization's website usually consists of many pages. The first page you come to when you type in an URL is called the "home page." This page usually contains a menu for the entire site and lets you know something about the site's creators and purpose. The home page contains links to other pages within that site, and often to other sites of interest. With most browsers you can go back to a previous link by clicking a button that says "Go Back;" you will not get "stuck" someplace you don't want to be, so don't be shy about exploring links.

Websites can be developed by any person or organization on any topic. The amount of information available on the Web today is staggering and continues to grow. You can utilize the Web for general research, as an educational tool, as a shopping mall, to find a long lost friend, get a new job, or answer most any question you might have; you are limited only by your imagination.

**Search Engines**

Now that you have a basic idea of the workings of the WWW, how do you go about finding websites that may interest you? A good starting point is to use one of the popular directories on the Web called search engines. A search engine allows you to type in keywords on the topic that you are interested in, and it will retrieve many sites that contain that word.

Some of the larger and more popular search engines are:

*Yahoo! - http://www.yahoo.com
*Alta Vista - http://altavista.digital.com
*Excite - http://www.excite.com
*Hot Bot - http://www.hotbot.com
*Lycos - http://www.lycos.com
*Infoseek - http://www.infoseek.com
*WebCrawler - http://webcrawler.com

To use a search engine, type in one of the addresses listed above. When the home page for that site comes up you will notice a "search" box in which you can type a key word or phrase. The site will then bring up all the information that it has available on that topic as a list of sites. Sometimes you will need to narrow your search; for example if you type "health" you may have thousands of site listings returned. On the other hand, if you are too specific, you may not have any sites returned as a result of your inquiry. This does not necessarily mean that these sites do not exist.

*Exercise:* Choose one of the following topics:

Protease inhibitors

Free radicals

Biofeedback

Now run your topic through three of the search engines listed above. How many hits do you get with each search engine? Do they seem like "quality hits" that you might be able to use if you were researching this topic? Now try to think of another way to get at the same topic—can you rephrase it, or search a related topic and get a better selection of hits? Can you find a way to narrow down your search?

_____

_____

_____

_____

**Bookmarks**

Once you find a website you will want to return to again in the future, you can "bookmark" it. To bookmark a site, go to that site, and after it has finished loading, choose "bookmark, " or "favorites" from your menu bar and your browser will instantly record the address to that site in your bookmark folder. Anytime you want to return to that site, you simply open the bookmark folder and click on the title of that website.

## Tips for Using the World Wide Web

- Be patient. Accessing websites can take time depending on how elaborate the site is, how fast your modem can download the information, and what time of day you might be surfing. You can speed things up a bit by turning off the "auto load image" option in your browser.

- Keep in mind that "hiccups" can occur in the transfer process. Sometimes the server of the website you are trying to reach may be down, there may be a lot of activity on that site, or there may be line noise. Just try again to load the website, or try again later.
- Because the Web is so dynamic, sites and links change every day. You might find some links on webpages that go nowhere, if the link has moved their pages to a new server or address.
- Remember that while the Web is a great source of information, not everything on it is true. It is up to you to evaluate the information you get from the Web; see the section on "Thinking Critically about Information on the Internet," page 15.

## **Listservs**

Listservs are electronic mailing discussion groups that take place through e-mail. They are groups of people who "get together" online to discuss a specific topic. There are listservs on nearly every topic imaginable. Here's how it works:

- You find out about a listserv dealing with a subject that you are very interested in discussing with others (i.e. treating HIV). Information on some health-related listservs appear on websites listed later in this booklet, or try a master list of listservs such as Lizst.
- In order to get involved in a discussion group, you have to subscribe to it. To subscribe, you send an e-mail to that mailing list's listserv with the word "subscribe" in the subject line and in the main body of the text. Also include your e-mail address.
- Usually, the listserv will then subscribe you to the list and send you instructions on how to "post" to the group. "Posting" means that you send out a comment to the entire mailing list that you have subscribed to.
- Every time any member posts to the listserv, all the subscribers get that posting as an e-mail message in their mailbox.

- Once you have subscribed you will begin to receive e-mail messages from the mailing list. Be careful though, some discussion groups have a large following and you may find your mailbox filling up faster than you can read the messages.

*Exercise:* Subscribe to a listserv on a topic you are interested in for one week, then unsubscribe. How many e-mails do you receive from the listserv in a week? Are the exchanges scholarly, or for a general audience? Are the exchanges usually civil, or do subscribers "flame" each other? What did you learn from reading the exchanges?

_____

_____

_____

_____

## **Newsgroups/Usenet**

Newsgroups, like listservs, are a way of discussing topics over the Internet with other people who share the same interests. However, newsgroups take place on an entirely different "network" called Usenet.

Usenet is composed of thousands of discussion areas called newsgroups. Individual comments that people make to one another on a newsgroup are called articles. You "post an article" when you want to make a comment. The lines of discussion within a newsgroup are called threads. To read the discussions on any newsgroup you must have software program called a newsreader.

Generally, your ISP will provide you with a newsreader program as part of the software package. When you open the newsreader it should download any new newsgroups that have been added. You can look through the entire list and choose which newsgroups interest you. When you find one of interest, you just open it up and begin reading the articles.

Newsgroup addresses are called hierarchies. Listed below are some of the standard hierarchies with an example of each. There are many other categories, some of which are from foreign countries.

alt - groups generally alternative in nature (such as alt.education.distance, alt.alien.visitors)

bionet - groups discussing biology and biological sciences (i.e. bionet.general, bionet.immunology)

comp - groups discussing computer or computer science issues (i.e. comp.infosystems)

misc - groups that don't fit into other categories (i.e. misc.fitness, misc.jobs)

news - groups about Usenet itself (i.e. news.groups)

rec - groups discussing hobbies, sports, music, and art (i.e. rec.food, rec.humor)

sci - groups discussing subjects related to the science and scientific research (i.e. sci.med.nursing, sci.psychology)

soc - groups discussing social issues including politics, social programs, etc. (i.e. soc.culture, soc.college)

talk - public debating forums on controversial issues (i.e. talk.abortion, talk.religion)

Before you make a posting to a newsgroup, you may want to "lurk" for awhile, that is, read the discussion without contributing your own posting. Lurking will give you a sense of the kinds of postings that are appropriate for that newsgroup and what the newsgroup culture is like.

People from all over the world, including some experts in the field may frequent newsgroups. They can be a great source of current information and of community. For example, a person suffering from a relatively rare disorder may not know anyone else with the same problems and concerns on campus or in town, but he or she can frequent a newsgroup specifically for people with that disorder to learn about other peoples' experiences, the latest treatments, and just to commiserate. However, be aware that not everything posted to a newsgroup is necessarily true; you must be a critical thinker.

*Exercise:* Browse the messages in the following newsgroups:

sci.med.diseases.cancer

alt.support.cancer

talk.politics.medicine

sci.med.immunology

>What kinds of things are discussed in each group? How would you describe the tone and level of discussions? What kind of person would benefit most from each newsgroup?

_____

_____

_____

_____

_____

## FTP

FTP stands for "File Transfer Protocol." FTP is a means by which you can send and receive (upload and download) documents and software over the Internet. FTP sites house these documents and software.

## Netiquette

Netiquette is simply the etiquette of the Internet. Because no one owns or polices the Internet, it is especially important that all users take responsibility for keeping communications civilized. Remember that the written communications of the Internet cannot convey meanings by voice inflection or body language, and it's easy to be misinterpreted.

Here are some good netiquette principles to keep in mind:

- Don't assume your correspondents know you are kidding, or being sarcastic, or anything else.
- Don't be too harsh or judgmental with those you disagree with.
- Don't use all capital letters; this may be interpreted as SCREAMING.
- Don't gossip or spread rumors on the Internet. This is a good way to get into trouble.
- Do proofread your messages before you send them.
- Do be kind and thoughtful in your correspondence.
- Do be honest; if you put misinformation onto the Net it could go to thousands of people.
- Do reply quickly to your correspondents.
- Do make messages and postings brief and to the point.

## Flaming

If you frequent the Net, and in particular newsgroups, you may get "flamed" or see someone else get flamed. Flaming is hostile response that generally occurs as a result of a disagreement and is meant to humiliate and upset the target. Often it is a direct personal attack. Just be forewarned and try not to stoop to that level, it isn't worth it.

## Emoticons

Emoticons are a fun way to express your feelings in electronic communication. They are a series of keystrokes and symbols that make a sideways picture. Emoticons can communicate to your reader that you are joking, disgusted, flirting, or sad—emotions that are otherwise hard to express in typewritten communication.

Here are some examples; tilt your head to the left.

:-)     this is the most common emoticon, known as a "smiley"
;-)     here is the smiley, winking
:-p     here is the smiley, sticking out its tongue
(:^)    here is a bald smiley
:-(     this is a sad smiley

## **Doing Research with the Internet**

The Internet is a great source of information for students doing research. There is no one "right" way to do research with the Internet, though it is important to stay focused; it's easy to lose hours of study time surfing the Net. Let's say you need to research a paper on cocaine addiction for your health class. A logical place to start might be to look at the addresses listed in the Resources section of this guide. Here you will find Web addresses for national and government organizations like the National Clearinghouse for Alcohol and Drug Information, and the National Institute on Drug Abuse. These sites contain links to other sites containing journal articles, research studies, and other information that will help you with your paper. Or, you can run a keyword through a search engine—in this case, "cocaine" or "cocaine and addiction," to narrow down the field.

The Web also contains lots of reference materials like dictionaries, atlases, maps, and directories. There are some services on-line that allow you to ask questions of experts like librarians and teachers. Be creative in your use of the Net as a resource—it will pay off.

You may also find valuable information in newsgroups or listservs. But, as always, be discriminating about the information you get from the Internet (see the next section). And you may not be able to do all your research on the Net—there is still quite a bit of information you can only find in your library.

It is good form to cite Internet sources as you would cite any research source. You can find several citation styles outlined on the Web; here is an example of a citation in APA style:

Wainwright, C. William (No date). *Stress and Working Parents* [Online]. Available: http://www.wainwright.edu [1997, July 14]

## **Thinking Critically about Health Information on the Internet**

When you have access to the Internet, you have an incredible amount of information at your fingertips. But remember that the Internet is not regulated, and anyone can post information there—accurate or inaccurate, helpful or misleading. The following tips will help you make sure the information you're getting is legitimate.

- Consider the source. Webpages maintained by government agencies, reputable schools, professional organizations, and major organizations like the American Heart Association can generally be trusted. Many other groups and individuals post accurate information, as well. But it is up to you to use your skepticism and common sense about any information you find on the Net, and always be aware of the source of your information.
- Know where you are. Even if you start out in a trustworthy site, the click of a button can catapult you into a completely different one. Learn to read your Web address (URL) so you know when you've left one site and entered another.
- Watch for red flags. The same common sense you'd use to evaluate any information applies doubly on the Internet. There are quacks on the Internet who prey on people who are desperate for answers about their health condition. And be especially careful about sending money to anyone with promises that sound too good to be true.

- Get a second opinion. To get more perspective on a piece of information, pick a key phrase or name and run it through a search engine to find other discussions of the topic. Post a query in a newsgroup and, of course, ask around at your school.

# INTERNET RESOURCES FOR HEALTH AND WELLNESS

## General Health Information

There is quite a bit of health information on the Internet, and the following sites and search engines will give you good jumping-off points for searches on just about any topic. The most reliable sites are those sponsored by the government, universities and medical centers, and disease-specific organizations.

**Centers for Disease Control and Prevention**

http://www.cdc.gov

This site includes a wide variety of materials, including national health statistics, information on HIV infection, travelers' health information, and the government's nutrition recommendations. It is also a gateway to specific CDC agencies.

**National Health Information Center (NHIC)**

http://nhic-nt.health.org/

This site puts people with health-related questions in touch with the organizations that are best able to provide answers to those questions. It has data on over 100 organizations that provide health information as well as an extensive list of toll-free phone numbers.

**Yahoo Health Directory**

http://www.yahoo.com/health

This site contains hundreds of health-related web sites covering a wide range of topics and a search engine to help you zero in on sites of interest.

**Achoo Health Directory**

http://www.achoo.com/

This site includes a searchable database of thousands of health-related sites.

**Go Ask Alice**

http://www.alice.columbia.edu/index.html

This site, sponsored by the health education and wellness program at Columbia University Health Service, provides a searchable, interactive, question and answer service. Both Professional and Peer educators provide answers to student questions about sexuality, weight control, stress, and many other health-related topics of interest to college students.

**Healthfinder**

http://www.healthfinder.or/default.htm

This site is a gateway to consumer health and human services information available from the U. S. government. It includes a large searchable database of websites, online publications, databases, support and self-help groups, and government and nonprofit health organizations.

**Health A to Z**

http://www.HealthAtoZ.com

Another searchable database of health information sites, with sites rated for quality.

**Duke University Diet and Fitness Center Home Page**

http://dmi-www.mc.duke.edu/dfc/home.html

This site provides scientific information on counseling to improve overall health and lifestyle.

**Healthy People 2000**

http://odphp.osophs.dhhs.gov/pubs/hp2000/

This Department of Health and Human Services site includes a list of all the Healthy People 2000 objectives, progress reviews, and priority areas. Recently, the site has been updated with the first draft of the Healthy People 2010 objectives, which has gone out for public comment.

**Dr. Koop's Community**

http://www.drkoop.com

Run by former Surgeon General C.Everett Koop, Koop's Community is dedicated to educating the consumer in order to empower them to improve their health. The site contains a list of forty disorders with in depth articles on symptoms, treatments, and organizations, a health search and health forums.

**Notes:**

## Aging

Americans today are living longer than ever before, and the study of aging is a growing science. If you are a traditional college-age student, you may not think much about aging. But we are all aging all the time, and choices you make now will affect your health and well being as you grow older. Chances are that at some point you will be called on to offer care or support to an older friend or relative. The following resources offer information on aging, diseases that may come with aging, and caregiving to the elderly.

**Caregiver Survival Resources**

http://www.caregiver911.com/

This site provides support and resources for people caring for the elderly. It includes a listing of national, regional, and local resources, survival tools, "Ask Dr. Caregiver," and an on-line chat group.

**Administration on Aging**

http://www.aoa.dhhs.gov/

This Department of Health and Human Services site contains links for students, health care professionals, seniors, and their families on aging-related topics.

**The Alzheimer's Page**

http://www.biostat.wustl.edu/alzheimer

Maintained by Washington University in St. Louis, this page contains information on Alzheimer's disease, an archive of their Alzheimer mailing list, and resources for caregivers.

**The National Council on the Aging**

http://www.ncoa.org/

This site includes information on political issues of concern to seniors, financial planning, tips on reentering the workforce, and health promotion.

**University of Texas Medical Branch Center on Aging**

http://www.utmb.edu/aging/

Contains information on health and aging, long-term care and housing, senior support services, caregiver support services, staying active after retirement, and much more.

**Newsgroups**

alt.support.alzheimers
bionet.neuroscience.amyloid

**Notes:**

## AIDS and HIV

The advent of protease inhibitor drugs seems to mark the beginning of a new era in the history of the HIV and AIDS epidemic around the world. But it is very important to realize that these drugs are not a cure for the disease, and that HIV prevention is as important as ever. HIV and AIDS are very well documented topics on the Internet. In addition to statistics, research, and information on prevention, there are support communities for people living with HIV and their families and loved ones.

### CDC National AIDS Clearinghouse

http://www.cdcnac.org/

This site contains information on the very latest HIV/AIDS treatments, youth public service announcements, a searchable database of all National AIDS Clearinghouse documents, as well as information in Spanish.

### The CDC HIV/AIDS Page

http://www.cdc.gov/diseases/hivqa.html

This Centers for Disease Control site contains information on preventing the spread of HIV/AIDS, and weekly morbidity and mortality reports for the disease.

### Harvard AIDS Institute

http://www.hsph.harvard.edu/hai

This site contains very highly specialized scientific and medical information on HIV/AIDS, conference proceedings, prevention information, images, and epidemiological information.

**HIV InSite**

http://kali.wcsf.edu

Maintained by the University of California at San Francisco, this site is packed with information on prevention, social issues, statistics, resources, and frequent updates on the latest information on the fight against HIV.

**HIV Infoweb**

http://www.infoweb.org

This site features a searchable library of information on HIV/AIDS. There is information on prevention and education, treatment information, current drug trials, and legal information for people affected by HIV/AIDS.

**Newsgroups**

sci.med.aids
misc.health.aids
alt.sex.safe

**Notes:**

## Alcohol

The death of Britain's Princess Diana in a drunk driving car crash highlighted once again the tragic consequences problem drinking can have. But it also seems we get mixed messages from the media. Is red wine really good for you? Is getting drunk on the weekend okay? When does social drinking cross the line into problem drinking? What are the effects of alcoholism on family members? The issue of alcohol use on college campuses is getting a lot of attention, and college students are finding ways to organize against alcohol oriented socializing. The following Internet sites offer various facts and figures about alcohol use and alcoholism, but few portray the intensely personal effects that alcohol use has on individual lives.

**Alcoholics Anonymous**

http://www.alcoholics-anonymous.org

This site contains information about alcoholism and Alcoholics Anonymous programs and literature.

**National Institute on Alcohol Abuse and Alcoholism**

http://www.niaaa.nih.gov/

This government site focuses on research and education related to alcohol use and abuse.

**National Association for Children of Alcoholics**

http://www.health.org/nacoa/

This site contains facts about children of alcoholics and resources on where to find support.

**Web of Addictions**

http://www.well.com/user/woa

This site includes in-depth information on alcohol and other drug abuse and addiction for anyone who needs factual information.

**Al-Anon/Alateen**

http://al-anon.alateen.org

This site provides information to family members of alcoholics and young people affected by alcoholism. It also contains support addresses and phone numbers.

**Habitsmart**

http://www.cts.com/crash/hbtsmrt

This site features an on-line self-scoring alcohol use assessment, tips for outsmarting cravings, and links to other sites on addiction.

**Newsgroups**

alt.recovery
clari.news.alcohol

**Notes:**

## Birth Control and Abortion

Most college students are aware that unprotected sex can and does lead to unwanted pregnancy. But making decisions about birth control can be confusing. Methods of contraception vary greatly in effectiveness, cost, convenience, and side effects, and no one method is best for everyone. The following sites present information on methods of birth control and their pros and cons, where to get contraceptives, and information on abortion and abortion services.

**Planned Parenthood**

http://www.ppfa.org/ppfa/

This site provides information on family planning, contraception, abortion and counseling services and contains links to regional offices of Planned Parenthood.

**Ultimate Birth Control Links Page**

http://gynpages.com/ultimate/

This site contains information on many different methods of birth control and decision-making strategies regarding contraception.

**Association of Voluntary and Safe Contraception International**

http://www.avsc.org/contraception/cperm.html

Maintained by an international non-profit agency, this site provides current information on birth control options, what's new in contraception and links to related sites.

**National Abortion Federation**

http://www.prochoice.org/

This site provides information on abortion and referrals, plus pro-choice political updates and information on how to get involved.

**National Abortion and Reproductive Rights League**

http://www.naral.org/

Information on the politics of the pro-choice movement.

**National Right to Life Committee**

http://www.nrlc.org/

Information on alternatives to abortion and the politics of the pro-life movement.

**Newsgroups**

talk.abortion
alt.support.abortion

**Notes:**

## Cancer

The word "cancer" strikes fear into the heart of many people, yet most of us are not aware of what we can do now to minimize our risk of getting cancer later. Lifestyle habits we develop in our youth, such as not smoking, eating a healthy diet, and minimizing exposure to the sun, can help us decrease our cancer risk as we age. The Web is a great source of information on cancer prevention, and also of medical and treatment information for all kinds of cancer. There are also several on-line support groups for people with cancer.

**American Cancer Society**

http://www.cancer.org

This site contains lots of information about cancer and the text of ACS fact sheets and other publications.

**National Cancer Institute**

http:www.nci.nih.gov/

This site offers a range of reliable government information on cancer, including research, statistics, support resources, and frequently asked questions.

**Cancerlink**

http://peronal.u-net.com/~njh/cancer.html

Cancerlink is a resource for cancer patients, family, and caregivers that features message boards, mailing lists, and an extensive list of links for organizations, hospitals, universities and more.

**Med Help International/Cancer Library**

http://www.medhelp.org/hom.htm

This site contains a searchable index with links to the text hundreds of articles relating to many different kinds of cancer.

**OncoLink/The University of Pennsylvania Cancer Center Resource**

http://cancer.med.upenn.edu/

Maintained by The University of Pennsylvania Cancer Resource Center, this site contains lots of information on cancer—its causes, symptoms, screening tests, prevention, and the answers to frequently asked questions.

**Newsgroups**

sci.med.diseases.cancer
alt.support.cancer
alt.support.cancer.prostate
alt.support.cancer.breast

**Notes:**

## Cardiovascular Health

Cardiovascular disease, including heart attacks and strokes, are the leading causes of death in the United States; over one-third of college students will die of cardiovascular disease. While heredity plays a role in determining who will get cardiovascular disease, lifestyle factors also play a big role. People who don't smoke, maintain a healthy weight, eat a balanced, lowfat diet, and who have social support are at less risk of dying of a heart attack. While there is little disagreement about these risk reducers, other recommendations are less clear cut. Recently there has been news advocating taking aspirin, fish oil, and red wine to prevent heart attacks. The following sources are well-respected organizations that can help you put the cardiovascular disease issue in perspective.

**American Heart Association**

http://www.amhrt.org

This site offers information on hundreds of topics relating to cardiovascular health and disease, including prevention, nutrition, smoking cessation, other lifestyle considerations, and cardiorespiratory endurance exercises.

**Heart and Stroke Foundation of Canada**

http://www.hsf.ca/

Contains general information, statistics on cardiovascular disease in Canada, a featured research article, information on food that's heart healthy, and a glossary.

**Determining and Reducing Your Risk**

http:www.heartinfo.com/detrisk.htm

This site lists risk factors for heart disease, blood and genetic tests used for heart disease screening, and ways of reducing your risk for heart disease.

### The Heart: An Online Exploration

http://www.fi.edu/biosci/heart.html

This interesting site, developed by the Franklin Institute of Science, provides an interactive multimedia tour of the heart. It also includes statistics, activities, and many resource materials and links.

### Cardiovascular Institute of the South

http://www.cardio.com

CIS is one of the leading institutes researching the diagnosis and treatment of cardiovascular disease. This site contains a searchable index of hundreds of doctor articles on various symptoms, treatments, and complications associated with cardiovascular disease.

### Cut to the Heart

http://www.pbs.org/wgbh/pages/nova/heart/

These pages supplement a PBS special on heart disease and include multimedia illustrations of heart function, information on pioneers of heart surgery, and the current treatments for heart disease.

### Newsgroups

sci.med.cardiology

**Notes:**

## Death and Dying

While death has always been a part of life, it seems to be getting more complex in our modern society. Issues about the right to die, physician-assisted suicide, organ donation, and appropriate care for the dying are making headlines and affecting countless families. The following resources present different points of view on these issues and offer resources for those faced with end-of-life decisions. The Internet can also be a source of support for those grieving the death of a loved one.

### Choice in Dying

http://www.choices.org/

Choice in Dying is a nonprofit group dedicated to fostering communication about end-of-life decisions. This site contains information on legal issues, news updates, publications, and advance directives for every state.

### The Compassionate Friends

http://longhor.jut.com/~tcf_national

The Compassionate Friends is a group offering support to people grieving the death of a loved one, especially a child. The site contains information on regional support groups, books on death and dying, and how to cope with grief.

### Hemlock Society USA

http://www.hemlock.org/hemlock/index.html

This group advocates the legalization of physician-assisted dying for the terminally ill. The site contains background information on the group and its position, information on legislative matters, and special resources for doctors and patients.

**Hospice Hands**

http://hospice-cares.com

This site provides information on hospice care for the dying, including a list of frequently asked questions, many links, hospice statistics, related organizations and consumer resources, and how to find a hospice.

**Newsgroups**

alt.support.grief
soc.support.pregnancy.loss

**Notes:**

## Environmental Health

We often hear that we are in an environmental crisis, but it can be hard to know what to do with this information. How does the environment affect individual health? And what can one individual do to help the environment? For starters, e-mail your congressperson about environmental issues that concern you! College students are tomorrow's leaders in environmental issues, and the following Web sites are just a few of the many offering health, scientific, and political information on environmental issues.

### American Environmental Health Foundation

http://www.aehf.com/

This nonprofit organization's site contains educational information on environmental health sensitivity issues and a listing of products of interest to those concerned with environmental health, such as pollution detection kits and water filtration systems.

### The Envirolink

http://envirolink.org/

This site connects to an extensive web of information and links related to environmental issues. Coverage includes ways individuals can reduce their impact on the environment, low-impact products and businesses, and a clearinghouse of information from many organizations worldwide.

### Directory of Sites in Occupational and Environmental Health

http://www.med.ed.ac.uk/hew/links/

This is a regularly updated directory of Web links to sites on health, the environment, and the workplace. Section headings include Hot Topics, Governmental, Educational, Toxicological, Pollution, Societies, and Directories.

**Environmental Protection Agency**

http://www.epa.gov

This site contains tons of information from the government, including environmental laws and regulations, EPA projects, resources for concerned citizens, businesses, and regions.

**Natural Resources Defense Council**

http://www.nrdc.org

The NRDC is dedicated to protecting Earth's natural resources through advocacy and exercising voting rights to make national and international governmental change relative to environmental issues. The NRDC On-Line contains articles on specific species of animals, clean air and water issues, among other hot topics. In many cases, information on how to contact government agencies is included, to offer you the opportunity to voice your opinion.

**Notes:**

## Exercise and Fitness

While surfing the Internet isn't the best form of exercise, there is a lot of information on fitness on the Web. You can find information on training, stretching, planning an exercise program, and avoiding injury. The Internet is also a great way for athletes to communicate about upcoming events, find out about local clubs and organizations, and investigate products and services related to fitness.

### The Fitness Partner Connection Jumpsite

http://www.primusweb.com/fitnesspartner/

This comprehensive site is a resource of fitness-related information on the Internet, including a searchable Fitness Library, a Calorie Calculator, and a Feature of the Month.

### The Internet's Fitness Resource

http://rampages.onramp.net/~chaz/

This site contains fitness information on many topics including fitness planning, products, sport-specific information, and special topics such as exercise and pregnancy.

### President's Council on Physical Fitness and Sports

http://www.hoptechno.com/book11.htm

This page outlines the guidelines for developing a personal exercise program, including checking your baseline health, workout schedules, measuring your heart rate, and controlling your weight.

**Worldguide Online**

http://www.worldguide.com/Fitness/

This site provides information about various types of cardiorespiratory endurance exercises and how to treat exercise injuries.

**Stretching Information**

http://www.enteract.com/~bradapp/docs/rec/stretching_1.html

This site provides answers to many frequently asked questions about stretching and flexibility. It includes information on types of stretching exercises, the physiology of stretching, and normal ranges of joint motion.

**American College of Sports Medicine (ACSM)**

http://www.a1.com/sportsmed/

This professional organization provides information on research projects, upcoming events, and issues related to sport safety and medicine.

**Newsgroups**

misc.fitness
misc.fitness.aerobic
alt.fitness.marketplace

**Notes:**

## The Health Care System

The 1990s have been a decade of crisis for our health care system. Spiraling health care costs, the problem of the uninsured, and the advent of managed care all mean that the way most of us approach health care is changing. Under the new systems it is more important than ever for consumers to be well-informed about their options, and for each of us to take control of our own health. These Web resources can help you research your health care options and make you a more confident and assertive health consumer.

**MedAccess**

http://www.medaccess.com

This site contains a wealth of information about health care, including a searchable directory of health care facilities, information on diseases, the health care system, statistics, and a Health Quiz.

**MedScape**

http://www.medscape.com/

This site features articles of interest to health care consumers in a searchable database, including patient information, and information on managed care.

**Idea Central Health Policy Page**

http://epn.org/idea/health.html

Updated bimonthly, this collection of articles on health policy recently included "Medicaid and Managed Care," "Keeping an Eye on HMOs," and "Baby Boomers and Medicare" and many others plus an archive of previous articles.

**Adverse Drug Interaction Search Engine**

http://csmctmto.interpoint.net/didx/public.html

This unique and helpful site allows users to input two or more drugs they may be taking and get feedback on possible interactions between them. It also includes a more detailed version of the search engine for physicians and other professionals.

**The Alternative Medicine Homepage**

http://www.pitt.edu/~cbw/altm.html

This site is a source of links to information on alternative medicine plus a link to the Office of Alternative Medicine and mailing lists and newsgroups.

**Notes:**

## Mental Health

Beware! According to the American Psychological Association, surfing the Internet can be addictive! But other mental health problems are much more common, and the Internet is a good source of information on mental disorders. Many people may feel reluctant to get assistance for a psychological problem, and the following pages may help in understanding those problems. There are psychologists and other therapists operating on the Internet in addition to the many support groups for people suffering from mental disorders. However keep in mind that the Internet is seldom a substitute for face-to-face psychological counseling.

### National Institute of Mental Health (NIMH)

http://www.nimh.hih.gov/home.htm

This government site contains helpful information about anxiety, depression, eating disorders, and other challenges to mental health.

### Psych Central, Dr. John Grohol's Mental Health Page

http://www.grohol.com

A guide to psychology, support, and mental health issues, resources, and people on the Internet.

### Internet Mental Health

http://www.mentalhealth.com/

This is an encyclopedia of mental health information, including medical diagnostic criteria, descriptions of mental disorders, and common medications to treat mental disorders.

**American Psychological Association**

http://www.apa.org

This professional organization provides information on mental health and illness, education and training, and topics of interest to mental health professionals.

**National Depressive/Manic-Depressive Association**

http://www.ndmda.org/

This site contains information on these disorders, including support groups, education, advocacy, suicide, adolescent depression, and success stories.

**Newsgroups**

alt.support.anxiety-panic
alt.support.depression
alt.support.loneliness
alt.support.sleep-disorders
soc.support.depression.crisis
soc.support.depression.family
soc.support.depression.manic
soc.support.depression.misc
soc.support.depression.seasonal
soc.support.depression.treatment
alt.support.ocd
alt.support.schizophrenia
alt.support.shyness

**Notes:**

## Nutrition

It seems that we are flooded almost daily with news about nutrition, but American's eating habits are still atrocious. These amounts to a national health problem, since four of the ten leading causes of death in America--heart disease, cancer, stroke, and diabetes--are related to poor diet. The Internet offers many ways to rethink your diet. You can evaluate your food choices on-line, make an eating plan, look up the nutritional values of your favorite fast foods (gasp), get tips on changing your eating habits, find hundreds of healthy recipes, and chat with others interested in nutrition.

### FDA Center for Food Safety and Applied Nutrition

http://vm.cfsan.fda.gov/list.html

This government site provides a wide variety of informations on topics such as food labeling, food additives, and foodborne illness.

### USDA Food and Nutrition Information Center

http://www.nalusda.gov/fnic/

This site contains the complete text of the Dietary Guidelines for Americans, helpful hints for reading and understanding food labels, and information about the Center's educational materials.

### Diet Analysis Web Page

http://dawp.futuresouth.com/

This unique site allows the user to analyze the nutritional value of what they eat for a day. Users select from a large database of foods to compile a list of their food intake, and then the site will calculate the fat, cholesterol, sodium, vitamins, and other nutritional information.

**Fast Food Finder**

http://www.olen.com/food/

Users can select from fast food offerings from over dozen chain restaurants and see a display of the food's calories, fat, cholesterol, percentage of calories from fat, and sodium.

**Virtual Vegetarian**

http://www.vegetariantimes.com/

Maintained by Vegetarian Times magazine, this site features vegetarian recipes, and links to other vegetarian-related sites, remedies, and vegetarian voices.

**Ask the Dietitian**

http://www.hoptechno.com/rdindex.htm

This site gives answers to many questions on nutrition. Subjects addressed include popular diets, fast food, vitamins and minerals, supplements, children and nutrition, sports nutrition, plus many others.

**Center for Science in the Public Interest**

http://www.cspinet.org/

This site by a well-known nutrition advocacy group includes current and back issues of *Nutrition Action Healthletter*, a fat quiz, a special section with information for kids, plus links to other Internet sites.

**Meals Online**

http://www/meals.com

This site offers over 10,000 healthful recipes.

**Newsgroups**

sci.med.nutrition
alt.support.diet

**Notes:**

## Pregnancy and Childbirth

Getting pregnant and having a baby may seem like a simple thing, but it is far from simple for many people. Making decisions about if and when to start a family, coping with infertility, avoiding health risks, and deciding about how and where to give birth are all-important issues. These resources can help in these decisions with facts and information, and also by sharing other people's experiences.

### Labor and Birth Resources

http://www.childbirth.org/articles/labor.html

This site contains information on pain relief in labor, what to expect during childbirth, childbirth methods, and more practical information.

### Health Resource Directory

http://www.stayhealthy.com/hrdfiles/hrd00113.html

This site includes information on infertility resources and organizations.

### Pregnancy, Birth, and Beyond Resource Guide

http://www.monarch-design.com/baby/index.html

This site offers information and links related to birth, breastfeeding, and midwifery issues.

### Pregnancy, Reproduction, and Health Education

http://www.childbirth.org/

This site contains medical information and personal stories about all phases of pregnancy and birth.

### It's Just Another Baby

http://www.westnet.com/~crywalt/pregnancy/

No statistics, no facts and figures, just one couple's honest story about their experiences with infertility, pregnancy, and childbirth. Very charming.

### Newsgroups

sci.med.midwifery
sci.med.obgyn
alt.infertility.primary
alt.infertility.secondary
misc.health.infertility
soc.support.pregnancy.loss
alt.support.breastfeeding
alt.support.childfree

### Notes:

## Psychoactive Drugs

Internet resources on drugs span many disciplines--health, medicine, psychology, biology, law, and politics to name a few. While most people can agree that drug addiction is a problem in our society, there are many approaches to avoiding and treating this problem. These resources present some different viewpoints about psychoactive drugs and, as always, use your critical thinking skills when you approach information on this topic.

### National Institute on Drug Abuse

http://www.nida.hih.gov

This government site provides information on drugs and drug abuse, statistics, information on events and grants, and many links to other sites of interest.

### Higher Education Center for Alcohol and Other Drug Prevention

http://www.edc.org/hec/

This site is sponsored by an organization that provides nation-wide support for campus alcohol and illicit drug prevention efforts. It provides information about alcohol and drug abuse on campus and links to related sites. It also has an area designed specifically for students.

### Cocaine Anonymous World Services

http://www.ca.org/

This site includes literature for cocaine addicts, the professional drug treatment community, and contact information for CA support groups.

**Narcotics Anonymous**

http://users.aol.com/na4napa/na1.html

This site contains readings on drugs and addiction, and links to regional Narcotics Anonymous offices.

**National Organization for the Reform of Marijuana Laws**

http://www.natlnorml.org/

NORML is a group advocating changes in laws regarding marijuana. Their site contains information on medical uses for marijuana, hemp products, and legislative information.

**Newsgroups**

sci.med.cannabis
alt.support.recovery.na
alt.drugs
clari.news.drugs
talk.politics.drugs

**Notes:**

## Sexuality

Sexuality is definitely a hot topic on the Internet. None of these Websites feature sexually explicit materials, but rather they present a balanced and sex-positive approach. There are newsgroups for many sexuality-related topics; the listing below is just a sampler.

### The Kinsey Institute for Research in Sex, Gender, and Reproduction

http://www.indiana.edu/~kinsey/

The library resources, research, training, and publications of one of the first and most respected institutions doing sexuality research.

### The Society for the Scientific Study of Sexuality

http://www.ssc.wisc.edu/ssss

The SSSS is the oldest organization of professionals dedicated to studying sexuality. Research and grants available encourage students to study the topic.

### Healthy Sexuality

http://www.healthgate.com/healthy/sexuality/fs.index.html

This site has weekly articles on a variety of sexuality topics.

### Sexuality Information and Education Council of the United States (SIECUS)

http://www.siecus.org/

Activities and publications of a professional organization promoting research and education on human sexuality.

### Good Vibrations

http://www.goodvibes.com/gvindex.html

This women friendly, sex-positive store sells a wide variety of sex toys, books, videos, and other materials over the Internet, and even includes an on-line antique vibrator museum.

### Newsgroups

alt.support.impotence
clari.news.sex
alt.lesbian
alt.nudism
alt.politics.sex
alt.romance
alt.support.lesbigay
alt.support.transgendered

### Notes:

## Sexually Transmitted Diseases

After declining for many years, sexually transmitted diseases are making a comeback, especially among people under age 20. Using latex condoms or dental dams consistently and properly can significantly reduce the transmission of STDs, including HIV. These Web sites contain information on preventing STDs, their symptoms and treatment, research, and social policy topics.

### The Johns Hopkins University STD Page

http://www.med.jhu.edu/jhustd/

This comprehensive site contains information on specific STDs, patient education, current research, and even a page on STDs and the arts.

### Division of AIDS, STD, and TB Laboratory Research (DASTLR)

http://www.cdc.gov/ncidod/dastlr/dastlr.html

This site is part of the CDC's National Center for Infectious Diseases. It has information on diseases and links to other sites of interest.

### The Safer Sex Page

http://www.safersex.org/

This site features general information on safer sex, condom usage, sexual health, a forum, index, and links to other sites of interest.

### American Social Health Association

http://sunsite.unc.edu/ASHA

This site contains general information on STDs, answers to frequently asked questions, a glossary, legislative advocacy information, research, and information about STD hotlines.

**Newsgroups**

alt.support.herpes
alt.sex.safe

**Notes:**

## Stress

We all experience stress in our lives, and learning to control stress is one of life's big challenges. Out-of-control stress can lead to depression, school or work problems, and health problems. These pages will help you learn about the triggers of stress, the unhealthy ways many of us automatically respond to stressors, and healthier responses that help control stress.

**Stress Management**

http:/www.ivf.com/stress.html

This site contains information on knowing your optimal level of stress and stress management strategies.

**Stress Busters**

http://stressrelease.com/strssbus.html

A site dedicated to reducing workplace stress, including stress building beliefs and stress-busting techniques.

**Stress, Depression, Anxiety, Sleep Problems, and Drug Use**

http://www.teachhealth.com/

This informative site offers information on recognizing stress, a self-test for stress levels, the biological bases of stress, and stress management techniques.

**Trauma Info Pages**

http://gladstone.uoregon.edu/~dvb/trauma.htm

This site focuses on trauma and post-traumatic stress disorder, and includes general information, resources, and support groups for those affected.

## The International Society for Traumatic Stress Studies

http://istss.com/

This professional organization presents information on traumatic stress, some publications, and links.

## Newsgroups

alt.support.anxiety-panic


## Notes:

## Tobacco

Just about everyone now knows that smoking is very bad for you, yet millions of Americans continues to smoke. Why do so many people continue to light up? Why do so many teenagers take up the habit every day? And what can nonsmokers do to fight tobacco and help others kick the habit? The following pages contain plenty of ammunition (health *and* political) for anti-smoking crusaders, and also contain information for smokers on how to quit.

### CDC's Tobacco Information and Prevention Source Page

http://www/cdc.gov/tobacco/

Contains Surgeon General's reports, research, educational materials, and tips on how to quit smoking, and tips for kids and teens.

### Prevention Online

http://www.health.org/

The National Clearinghouse for Alcohol and Drug Information's Website contains educational and prevention-related material about tobacco.

### NicNet: Nicotine and Tobacco Network

http://www.acsc.arizona.edu/nicnet/

This well-done site features a searchable database of tobacco information, news, material on kids and tobacco, how to quit, research updates, and pro-tobacco points of view.

### Tobacco Control Resource Center

http://www.tobacco.neu.edu/

This site is presented by the Northeastern University School of Law and presents current information on litigation against the tobacco industry, the tobacco settlement, and the text of important legal documents related to tobacco.

## The Quitnet

http://www.quitnet.org/

This site contains interactive tools and questionnaires, support groups, a library, and the latest news on tobacco issues. Geared toward helping smokers quit.

## Smokescreen Tobacco Central Network

http://www. Smokescreen.org

This advocacy group for tobacco control's site allows you to type in your zip code and get information on your congressional representatives, their voting record on tobacco-related issues, and a record of the tobacco PAC money they've accepted.

## Medicine OnLine/environmental tobacco smoke

http://www.meds.com/mol/env_smk.html

This site contains information on environmental tobacco smoke—what it is and why it's dangerous.

## Newsgroups

alt.support.stop-smoking
alt.support.non-smokers
alt.support.non-smokers.moderated
clari.news.smoking

## Weight Management and Eating Disorders

Issues related to weight are often surrounded by intense personal feelings of guilt, longing, disgust, and anxiety. Millions of Americans, especially women, spend countless hours and dollars trying to achieve a "perfect weight." But there is a lot of hype and misinformation about weight and diets. The following sites will help you determine your healthy weight range, offer sensible tips on losing excess weight, and offer support to overeaters and those suffering from eating disorders.

### The Overeaters Recovery Group

http://www..hiwaay.net/recovery/

This site contains many links to online support for overeaters, including mailing lists and newsgroups.

### Overeaters Anonymous

http://www.overeatersanonymous.org/

This site introduces the 12-step program of Overeaters Anonymous, information on compulsive eating, regional services, and ways to find a meeting near you.

### Healthy Weight

http://healthyweight.com/

This comprehensive and attractive site features an on-line BMI calculator, information on weight management, a resource center, items in the news, and links.

### Cyberdiet

http://www.cyberdiet.com/

Another good site, this one includes assessment tools, an on-line nutritional profile, a daily food planner, a database of foods, a recipe index, and more.

### Light Cooking

http://www.lightcooking.com/

This site focuses on ways to cut fat and calories in your cooking and features recipes, cooking tips, a recipe conversion page, questions and answers, and a kid's corner.

### Eating Disorders

http://www.something-fishy.com/ed.htm

Contains information on anorexia and bulimia, personal stories, and links to support and recovery groups.

### Ask the Dietitian/Overweight

http://www.hoptechno.com/overweig.htm

This site gives questions and answers on many topics related to nutrition and weight control. Topics include how to limit fat intake, eating disorders, and fast food.

### Newsgroups

alt.support.obesity
alt.support.big-folks
alt.support.eating-diord

### Notes: